KING HENRY VIII

FRONT COVER: *Henry VIII, 1537. This magnificent portrait of the king from the school of Holbein is in the Walker Art Gallery, Liverpool.*
BACK COVER: *Henry VIII by Joos van Cleve, painted to commemorate the translation of the Bible in 1540.*
FACING PAGE: *This portrait after Holbein was painted in 1536, shortly after Henry's marriage to Jane Seymour, who became his third wife.*
ABOVE: *Henry VIII and his children, a Protestant allegory of the English Reformation. Edward VI kneels by his father's throne; Catholic Mary and her husband, Philip of Spain, are followed in by war; Protestant Elizabeth brings in peace and plenty.*

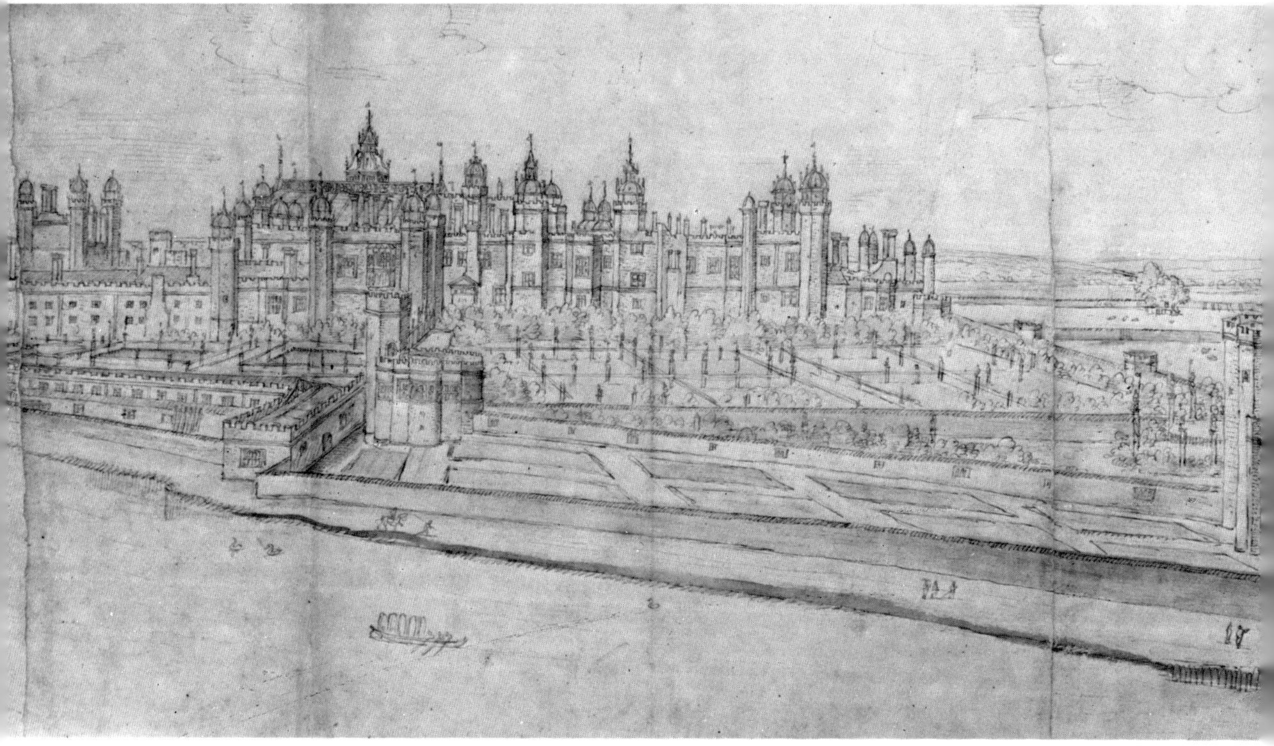

KING HENRY VIII

G. W. O. Woodward

IN our day Henry VIII is best remembered for having had six wives. To his own generation he was chiefly memorable, in the words of the chronicler Edward Hall, as the "Undoubted flower and very heir" of "the two noble and illustrious families of Lancaster and York" which had been "long in continual dissension for the crown of this noble realm." These two, apparently distinct, reasons for remembering Henry are in fact closely linked, for one of the forces which impelled the king into his earlier matrimonial crises was the urgency with which he felt the need, for the sake of the peace and security of his kingdom, to have a son to be his undoubted heir.

In Henry's day a great deal of uncertainty still surrounded the question of the rights of women in the matter of succession to the crown. That Henry's daughters, Mary and Elizabeth, would each in turn eventually occupy their father's throne, and that the only challenge to their titles would come from female rivals, could not be foreseen by the men of Henry's generation. All that they knew was that since the unhappy days of Matilda in the twelfth century no woman had so much as claimed, let alone sat upon, the English throne, and that there were many who were prepared to say that no woman could. They also knew that the "Wars of the Roses", though they had not begun as a dynastic quarrel, had later acquired that character, and that the conflict between the rival claims of York and Lancaster had come to turn upon the comparative merits of male and female descent from Edward III. Now Henry was, through his father Henry VII, heir to Lancaster, and, through his mother Elizabeth eldest daughter of Edward IV, heir to York, so that in his person the dynastic quarrel was for the time being healed. If he had a son to succeed him, that son would be gladly accepted by all without question as his proper heir. If he left behind him only daughters, or, worse still, no child at all, then the risk of a new dynastic dispute breaking out between the partisans of rival claimants was very great. The desire to avoid, if at all possible, any renewal of the civil strife of the previous century worked strongly upon Henry's mind and contributed significantly to the complexities of his marital history.

The "Wars of the Roses", it must also be remembered, did not end

Continued on page 5

* * *

FACING PAGE (above): *A contemporary drawing of the palace at Greenwich where Henry was born, 28th June 1491.*

FACING PAGE (below): *Hampton Court, built by cardinal Wolsey and acquired by the king after Wolsey's downfall in 1529. This engraving shows the riverside palace very much as it was in Henry's day.*

RIGHT: *The family of Henry VII with St. George and the Dragon, painted c. 1509. The king and his three sons, Arthur, Henry and Edmund are on the left, his queen, Elizabeth of York, and her daughters Margaret, Elizabeth, Mary and Catherine are on the right.*

ABOVE LEFT: *This portrait is probably of Prince Arthur, eldest child of Henry VII and Elizabeth of York. Born in 1486, he married Catherine of Aragon in 1501 and died less than five months later.*

ABOVE RIGHT: *Elizabeth of York, eldest daughter of Edward IV and sister of the Princes in the Tower. Her marriage to Henry VII, the heir of Lancaster* (facing page) *united the two houses which had for so long been at war. Henry VII's title to the throne did not depend upon his marriage, which took place after his coronation, but did help the reconciliation of Yorkist partisans to his 'usurpation'. In later reigns royal propagandists made much of this happy merging of the rival houses (symbolised in the blending of the red and white roses) of which Henry VIII was the fruit.*

LEFT: *Margaret Beaufort (1443–1509), mother of Henry VII, was the Tudor link with the House of Lancaster. Lady Margaret was a notable patroness of learning. She endowed chairs of divinity at both Oxford and Cambridge, and was a close associate of John Fisher and Erasmus.*

* * *

Other books in the Pride of Britain series of particular interest to students of the Tudor period are: *The Six Wives of Henry VIII; Sir Thomas More; Queen Elizabeth I; Mary Queen of Scots; Sir Walter Ralegh; John Knox; Hampton Court Palace; Britain's Kings and Queens; The Royal Line of Succession; The Dissolution of the Monasteries; H.M. Tower of London;* and *Prisoners in the Tower.*

abruptly in 1485 with the victory of Henry Tudor over Richard III at Bosworth. Though many of the supporters of the defeated house were pacified by the new king's marriage to Elizabeth of York, and now desired peace more heartily than any further party advantage, not all the subjects of the first Tudor king were content to accept his "usurpation" without protest. For the greater part of his reign Henry VII was troubled with conspiracies, rebellions and rival claimants to his throne. The year 1491, in which the future king Henry VIII was born at Greenwich on 28 June, saw also the beginning of the long career of the pretender Perkin Warbeck who, in his assumed character of Richard, duke of York and son of Edward IV, claimed a better right to the English throne than Henry VII. And Warbeck, who was until his capture at Beaulieu in 1497 a constant and serious threat, was not by any means the last rival claimant to trouble the house of Tudor. In 1501 Edmund de la Pole, earl of Suffolk, nephew of Edward IV and a genuine member of the house of York, suddenly fled abroad to the court of the emperor Maximilian, where he remained a potential source of danger until Maximilian's son Philip surrendered him to Henry VII in 1506. We must not ignore the effect upon young prince Henry of this atmosphere of dynastic insecurity in which he grew to manhood. It must be allowed a part in explaining, though not in excusing, the savagery he was later to display towards so many members of the house of York.

Henry VIII was the third child and second son of his parents. He was not, therefore, born to rule. The dynastic hopes of his father rested at first upon his elder brother Arthur, born in 1486. It was for Arthur that Henry VII worked so hard to obtain a Spanish bride. Under Ferdinand and Isabella the recently united kingdoms of Aragon and Castile were rapidly emerging as the foremost power in Europe. A matrimonial alliance with their rulers would add immeasurably to the prestige of the house of Tudor and demonstrate to the world that Spain accepted Henry VII as legitimate king of England. And so, in 1501, after lengthy negotiations and much shrewd bargaining on both sides, Catherine, the youngest daughter of the Spanish sovereigns, came to England to wed the young prince of Wales. The marriage was celebrated with great pomp in St. Paul's Cathedral on 14 November, and prince Henry ceremoniously escorted his brother's bride down the length of the church. Less than five months later, on 2 April 1502, prince Arthur was dead.

Henry, who was not yet eleven years old, thus suddenly became the heir to his father's throne, and before another year had passed it had become clear that upon him alone would now depend the very survival of the Tudor line. His younger brother Edmund had died in 1500 at the age of sixteen months. His two surviving sisters, Margaret, married to James IV of Scotland in 1503, and Mary, five years his junior, were discounted because of their sex. No more sons were born to Henry VII for, in February 1503 his queen, Elizabeth, died, shortly after giving birth to a girl who did not long survive her mother. And yet the future of the house of Tudor seemed to be in very good hands. Henry was a fine sturdy lad who was already making a name for himself not only for his physical prowess but also for his intellectual accomplishments. His father saw to it that he received a thorough training in French and Latin, the diplomatic languages of his day. He also developed a keen interest in and a modest talent for music, and a positive passion for theology. Making every allowance for the natural tendency of courtiers to flatter their prince, it is difficult to deny that Henry grew up to be a very talented and accomplished young man.

Continued on page 6

This royal paragon was only in his eighteenth year when, on 21 April 1509, his father died and he entered into his kingdom. Seldom in the history of England had a new reign begun under better auspices. The new king was young, healthy, intelligent, graceful and gifted. His kingdom was at peace. The nobility were tamed. No rival claimant appeared to challenge his accession. He inherited from his father a level-headed set of experienced councillors, and a credit balance in the treasury. His people admired him and were prepared to love him, and he could look forward to a long and prosperous reign. How was it then that this most promising prince degenerated by degrees into a savage and suspicious despot?

Ill-health had, of course, its contribution to make to the process of deterioration. The precise nature of the disease, or diseases, from which the king suffered in his last years cannot now be determined from the rather imprecise medical evidence available, but it is clear that his latter-day obesity was abnormal and incapacitating, and that, from about 1537 onwards, he suffered agonies from an ulcerated leg. Yet ill-health and physical suffering alone, though they

* * *

ABOVE LEFT: *Henry's Coronation Oath. The text of the oath was amended by Henry, to conform with his later views about the proper relationship of crown and church. Most significant alterations are: (i) The undertaking "to keep and maintain the right and the liberties of Holy Church of old time granted by the righteous Christian kings of England" is amended to read "to keep and maintain the lawful right and the liberties of old time granted by the righteous Christian kings of England to the Holy Church of England not prejudicial to his jurisdiction and dignity royal" (ii) A promise "to keep the peace of the Holy Church" becomes an undertaking to "endeavour himself to keep unity in his clergy and temporal subjects."*

BELOW LEFT: *The coronation of Henry and Catherine. This woodcut of 1509 is the earliest contemporary printed representation of an English coronation.*

FACING PAGE: *Queen Catherine of Aragon, Henry's first queen. Married first to his brother Arthur who died in 1502, she became Henry's wife and queen shortly after his accession in 1509. Though she bore Henry several children (only Mary I survived) she never provided the longed-for son. Divorced in 1533, she died in 1536.*

may shorten a man's temper and sap his energies, do not necessarily turn him into a pitiless tyrant. On the contrary, many a good man has made a virtue of ill-health and risen above his suffering with new-found strength of character. There is, therefore, more to the degeneration of Henry than illness alone. The weakness in his character which his illness brought out was there before his sufferings began. The supreme self-confidence of the gifted youth passed imperceptibly into a self-destroying pride which in turn gave place to an arbitrary and domineering wilfulness which made him impatient of the slightest check and furious at any frustration. Coupled with this was a considerable capacity for unconscious self-deception which most frequently manifested itself in the guise of a highly elastic conscience. It became in the end virtually impossible for him to distinguish what he wanted from what was right.

The tragedy of Henry VIII lies in the fact that it was his very abilities which could have made him a truly great king which were to be his undoing. Encouraged from his earliest days, by the adulation and flattery of courtiers and companions, to believe that there was no activity of mind or body at which he did not excel, and possessed before he was fully a man of the power to gratify his every whim, it is not really surprising that he so soon acquired an ineradicable sense of his own superiority, not only physically and mentally, but even spiritually, over all his fellow men. From believing that he possessed superior gifts it was but a short step to believing that he was a superior person, something more than mere man, participating somehow in the wisdom and infallibility of his Creator who had singled him out to govern his people and endowed him generously with the necessary abilities. To oppose the will of one who stood so close to God was to oppose the will of God himself.

While all went well for the young king these defects in his character lay concealed. And for nearly two decades all did, on the whole, go well for Henry. One of his first acts upon becoming king was to marry Catherine of Aragon, his brother Arthur's widow. Henry probably felt himself in honour bound to wed this Spanish princess to whom he had been betrothed within fifteen months of his brother's death, but the marriage would also be recommended to him by his councillors on grounds of policy. The Spanish alliance that went with it was too valuable to be lightly cast away. Henry VII and Ferdinand of Aragon, past masters of the diplomatic game, had haggled for six years over the details of this second Anglo-Spanish royal marriage. Henry VIII, with the impatience of youth, swept all difficulties aside, and positively hurried on the wedding. The problem created by the closeness of the relationship between the king and his intended bride had been dealt with by a bull of dispensation issued by Pope Julius II in 1503. There was no need to go into that matter again.

Catherine was five and a half years older than Henry, a young woman of twenty-three now marrying a youth of eighteen. The difference in their ages was not significant then, but came to be critical later. Catherine in her youth was, by the standards of her day, quite a beauty, and certainly very accomplished. Henry had every reason to be proud of his newly-crowned queen. The weeks that followed their marriage were filled with festivities of every sort, with masques, with jousting, with feasting and dancing, and Catherine joined as exuberantly in it all as ever Henry did. The court of the new king was certainly a gay one. Gone was the atmosphere of restraint and caution which had surrounded the widower Henry VII. Gone too was his careful penny-pinching, replaced by a generous liberality which seemed in contrast utterly extravagant. Rich clothes, sumptuous food, elaborate masquerades and disguisings were now the rule. Young ladies of breeding with good looks and lively manners were always welcome at court to enhance the revelries with their charms, but the king had eyes only for Catherine, and made in those early days a very public parade of his affection for his talented wife.

Continued on page 10

IMPERATOR MAXIMILIAN
HERICUS OCTAVUS REX ANGLIÆ

Terwaen
The Bataile of

ABOVE: *The king in parliament. A contemporary drawing of the scene at the opening of parliament in 1515. On the king's right hand sit the bishops and parliamentary abbots, on his left the lay peers. In the centre the judges sit on woolsacks and the clerks record the proceedings. In the foreground facing the king stands the speaker of the house of commons. Wolsey can be identified by the cardinal's hat above his head.*

★

ABOVE LEFT: *The meeting with Maximilian I. In 1513 the emperor and Henry VIII waged a joint campaign against France. To fight alongside this great prince was very flattering to Henry's vanity, and this painting records their meeting (bottom), their subsequent conference (centre) and their clash with the French (top).*

★

BELOW LEFT: *The battle of the Spurs, another incident in the Tournai campaign of 1513. It is so called because of the speed with which the French (on the right) left the field. Although but a small scale engagement it gave Henry much personal satisfaction, convincing him of his military prowess. The general confusion of the battle is well conveyed.*

Abroad as well as in his own kingdom, in his relations with his fellow monarchs and on the field of battle, king Henry also cut a very impressive figure. It is true that his first intervention in the current European conflict, the English expedition to Spain in 1512, was rather disgracefully unsuccessful, but the memory of that humiliation was quickly effaced by the triumphs of the following year, the defeat of the Scots at Flodden, the rout of the French at the Battle of the Spurs, and the capture of Tournai and Thérouanne. After all this Henry's international reputation stood high, and reached its peak in 1520 when his two great contemporaries, Francis I, king of France from 1515, and Charles V, king of Spain from 1516 and Holy Roman Emperor from 1519, competed eagerly for his support. This was the year of the Field of Cloth of Gold when Henry and Francis tried so hard to out-shine each other at a series of meetings in a specially constructed pavilion on the frontier between France and the English-held pale of Calais. It was also the year in which Henry had two meetings with the emperor Charles, one in England before he sailed to meet Francis, and the second at Gravelines in the Netherlands immediately after the Field of Cloth of Gold. There was much less ostentation about these meetings between the king of England and the Habsburg emperor, but they were much more productive of goodwill, and the Anglo-Habsburg alliance which Catherine, as Charles' aunt, represented in her own person, was very firmly cemented.

In 1521 Henry added to his domestic, diplomatic and military triumphs a distinction of another kind which gave him equal satisfaction. He turned theologian and author and produced, in his famous *Assertio Septem Sacramentorum,* an answer to some of the controversial writings of Martin Luther. Though the first draft may have been polished up a bit with the help of Sir Thomas More, there can be little doubt that the book was in the main Henry's own work. It did not rise much above the scurrilous level which at that time was thought appropriate to works of controversy, but it earned from Pope Leo X the grant of the title *Fidei Defensor* (Defender of the Faith) which Henry and all his successors have ever since proudly borne. Truly the king of England seemed destined to excel in everything to which he turned his hand.

Yet there were disappointments also, even in these early years. Chief of

* * *

LEFT: *Margaret Tudor, Henry's elder sister, married at the age of 13 to James IV of Scotland, and great-grandmother of James VI and I. Her husband was defeated and killed by her brother's troops at Flodden in 1513. Margaret's scandalous widowhood occasionally embarrassed even Henry.*

FACING PAGE (above left): *Sir Thomas More, the most famous Englishman of Henry's day who enjoyed an international reputation as a scholar. A faithful servant of the king as ambassador, speaker in Parliament, and lord chancellor, More resigned in protest against Henry's rejection of the pope. He was too eminent to be allowed to dissent in private from the new regime, and was executed as a traitor in 1535.*

FACING PAGE (above right): *Thomas Wolsey, lord chancellor, cardinal and archbishop of York. He rose rapidly in favour and was Henry VIII's right-hand man from 1512 to 1529. He fell from grace when he failed to solve the King's matrimonial difficulties and died at Leicester in 1530 en route to face further charges in London.*

these was the failure of Catherine to provide that much-needed son. Six times at least in the first nine years of married life the queen conceived. Once she miscarried, twice she went the full time but her baby was born dead. One boy lived for a few hours, another for seven and a half weeks. The only royal child to survive infancy was the princess Mary, born in 1516. The earlier of these domestic tragedies did not cause the king undue distress. Such occurrences were commonplace enough in an age when the infant mortality rate was very high, even in the families of kings where the best of contemporary medical skill was always available. Henry knew this only too well. Of his seven brothers and sisters four had died at birth or in early infancy, and his remaining brother, Arthur, had not survived his teens. On Catherine's side, the record was, if anything, worse. Of the ten children born to her mother only five had survived infancy, and two of those five had died comparatively young. So Henry had not at first any reason to be unduly anxious, and could console himself with the thought that he and his queen were young, and that there would be other children to come who would surely live. But steadily the mounting list of disappointments took their toll. Each time it was less easy to be confident about the future, and after 1518, though Catherine was only thirty-three, there seem to have been no more pregnancies.

Henry, like most of the kings and nobles of his day, did not confine his amorous exploits within the bonds of matrimony, and yet, when compared with some of his contemporaries, notably Francis I of France and James V of Scotland, he would appear to have been an exceptionally faithful husband. Only one illegitimate child of his is on record, and only two mistresses can be named with any degree of certainty. However, by 1520 the disparity in age between the king and his queen was beginning to tell. He was as full of youthful vigor as ever. She was worn down by repeated pregnancies and the many disappointments had told heavily on her spirits. She no longer participated so fully in the gay round of court festivities. She was not always even a spectator. She had lost most of her youthful zest, and was turning increasingly to more serious pursuits. She was often at her devotions. It was almost inevitable that Henry should have been tempted to infidelity.

Just when Anne Boleyn first came on the scene it is not easy to say with absolute certainty. As a young girl she had gone to France as one of the ladies-in-waiting to Henry's sister Mary when she had been married to Louis XII in 1514. Her royal mistress had returned to England the following year, but Anne had stayed on until the end of 1521 when the outbreak of war had obliged her to leave. The first positive indication that the Boleyns were becoming people of importance at court was given in 1525 when Anne's father was raised to the peerage as Viscount Rochford, but it is as likely as not that it was his other daughter Mary who had secured this distinction for him. It is not until 1527 that we can say for certain that Henry had fallen for Anne.

Continued on page 15

Henry VIII c. *1520*

BELOW: *An unfamiliar early portrait of Henry VIII, by an unknown artist. The king is about 30 years old, and his latter-day corpulence is not yet evident. There is a strong family resemblance to prince Arthur* *(see page 4).*

ABOVE RIGHT: *The scene at Dover as Henry embarked for France. The royal flagship in the centre is probably the* Henry Grace à Dieu, *one of the largest English ships afloat at the time.*

BELOW RIGHT: *The Field of Cloth of Gold. In 1520 England briefly held the balance of power between the two rival monarchs, emperor Charles V of Spain and Francis I of France. The alliance of England with either would almost certainly ensure the defeat of the other. This, therefore, was a year of intense diplomatic activity which saw two meetings between Charles and Henry, and sandwiched in between, the famous encounter between Francis and Henry at the Field of Cloth of Gold. A special pavilion was built on the French frontier, approximately half way between Boulogne and English-held Calais. The picture (below right) is again a narrative one, displaying many separate incidents as though they happened together. Henry and Wolsey can be seen arriving in procession. In the centre background Henry and Francis meet in a large tent. In the top right corner a tournament is being held. The fountain in the foreground is running with wine and some spectators have drunk too much.*

"Myne awne swethhart"

RIGHT: *A letter from Henry to Anne Boleyn in his own hand. "Myne awne swethhart, thes shall be to advertes yow off the grette alengenes* (loneliness) *that I fynde her*(e) *syns your departyng, for I ensure* (assure) *yow me thynkyth the tyme lenger syns your departyng now last then I was wonte to do a hole fortnyght. I thynke your kyndnes and my fervenes* (fervour) *off love causyth it for otherwyse I wolde not have thowght it possyble that for so littyll a wyle it shulde have grevyd* (grieved) *me. But now that I am comyng toward yow me thynkyth my painnys* (pains) *bene* (be) *halfe relesyd* (released) *and allso I am ryght well comfortyd in so muche that my boke makyth substantially for my matter, in lokying* (looking) *whereoff I have spente above iiii ours* (4 hours) *thys day, whyche causyd me now to wrytte the schortter letter to yow at thys tyme by cause off summe payne in my hed. Wyschyng* (Wishing) *myselfe specially a nevenynge* (of an evening) *in my swethart harmys* (arms) *whose pretty dukkys* (breasts) *I trust shortly to cusse* (kiss). *Wryttyn with the hand off hyme that was, is, and shalbe yours by hys wyll Hs.R." This letter, with others is in the Vatican Library.*

Meanwhile it is clear that the question of the succession had begun to worry the king. In 1525 he publicly acknowledged parentage of his illegitimate son, Henry Fitzroy, born some six years earlier, made him Duke of Richmond, and seemed to be preparing the way for making him his heir.

Here, in the king's dynastic anxieties and in his infatuation with Anne, we have the two principal reasons for his rejection of Catherine. It is hardly necessary to drag in Wolsey's diplomatic schemes. It is true that in 1526 he wanted to switch England from alliance with the Habsburgs to alliance with France, and it is also true that Catherine consistently used what influence she had on behalf of her nephew Charles. To have had Henry free to take a French princess to wife might well have suited Wolsey's immediate purpose, but would have involved the bastardising of the princess Mary for whom he was trying at that very time to secure a French husband. It is in any case inconceivable that even in the fullness of his pride the great cardinal would have presumed to have taken the initiative in trying to pull down the queen. Once it was clear that Henry was anxious to be rid of Catherine, then Wolsey could safely encourage and assist him, and even hope to take diplomatic advantage of the consequences, but he would hardly have dared to take the first step himself.

* * *

The long drawn-out proceedings in king Henry's "Great Matter" commenced in May 1527 when the two English archbishops cited the king to appear before them and answer to the charge of having lived in unhallowed union with his deceased brother's wife for almost eighteen years. This was consistently the line that Henry took, that he and Catherine had never been properly married so that he was free, as a bachelor, to marry whom he would. Only the supporting arguments changed. At first he pleaded that the bull of Pope Julius II, which had purported to remove the obstacle of affinity which had stood between him and Catherine, had been obtained under false pretences, and was therefore invalid. At a later stage he argued, more sweepingly, that no papal bull, however correctly obtained, had any power to set aside the divine prohibition against such marriages as his. Only in the very last stages of the affair did he, somewhat reluctantly, claim that the pope had no power in England at all.

While all these arguments occupied the lawyers and ambassadors, and while pope Clement VII tried desperately to find a solution that would satisfy the English king without outraging Catherine's powerful nephew Charles, Henry and Anne had to wait. It is often said that it was Anne who made Henry wait by refusing to yield to his advances until she was assured of the crown as queen, but Henry had good reasons of his own for being content with some delay. To have merely an illicit liaison with Anne would not have served his purpose. He wanted a legitimate son, and he intended Anne to be the mother of that son. For that he was prepared to wait, but not for ever.

Whether or not the story of the king's conscientious scruples was originally no more than a contrived

Continued on page 18

FACING PAGE (above left): *Thomas Cranmer, archbishop of Canterbury, who suggested that Henry's divorce case was for theologians not lawyers. He was the personal chaplain to Anne Boleyn and always exerted a moderating influence on Henry.*

FACING PAGE (above right): *Stephen Gardiner, lawyer, diplomat, politician and bishop of Winchester. Although he accepted the royal supremacy he was opposed to other changes and became the leader of the conservative faction in opposition to the protestant policies of Cranmer and Cromwell.*

RIGHT: *Anne Boleyn, Henry's second queen, who first attracted the king's attention in about 1527. Crowned in June 1533 she gave birth to Elizabeth in September and was executed for unfaithfulness in 1536.*

ANNO · ETATIS ·
· SVÆ · XLIX

And yet it is difficult to understand the savagery of Henry's final treatment of the woman who had once meant so much to him. It would have been enough either to have executed her (in a sycophantic and increasingly faction-ridden court it was never difficult to find persons prepared to supply sufficient damning "evidence"), or to have declared her marriage void (there were several grounds upon which it could most plausibly have been impugned). Was it really necessary to do both? So complete was Henry's revulsion from the woman he had once loved so passionately that her death alone was not enough. He must free his royal person of all taint of association with her, even at the cost of bastardising her daughter and imperilling the succession. Henry certainly made a clean sweep of the past in 1536. When, on 30 May that year, he married Jane Seymour, he was, in his own eyes, a bachelor with no legitimate offspring.

On this marriage, Henry's third, heaven at long last seemed to smile. On 12 October 1537 Jane gave birth to a prince, the future king Edward VI, and thus vindicated, in the king's view, all that he had said and thought about his previous marriages. Great was his jubilation, and for a few days all seemed set fair. Jane, however, never fully recovered from the birth, and on 25 October she was dead.

The death of Jane was followed by Henry's longest wifeless period in the whole of his reign. This in itself is a measure of the depths of his affection for his third queen. Her loss was a real blow to him and for a long time he had no thoughts of replacing her. She was, after those early idyllic days with Catherine of Aragon, the one he loved best of all his wives, and she is the one who shares his tomb at Windsor. Cynics, of course, will say that she was fortunate both to bear him a son and to die before he tired of her, but, be that as it may, more than two years were to pass before the sorrowing widower could bring himself to marry again.

This time he approached the question in a more orthodox fashion and sought to couple with marriage a diplomatic alliance with a ruling house. Under the guidance of Thomas Cromwell, who in the 1530s took over the role of chief minister which Wolsey

Continued on page 22

* * *

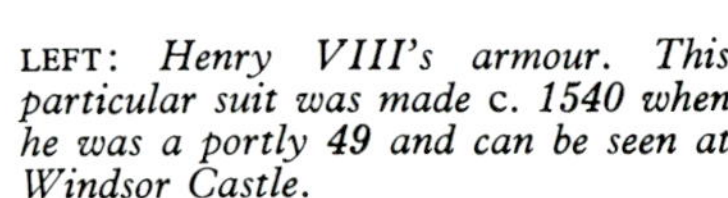

LEFT: *Henry VIII's armour. This particular suit was made* c. *1540 when he was a portly 49 and can be seen at Windsor Castle.*

FACING PAGE (above): *The king presenting a charter to the Barber-Surgeons. A group portrait by Holbein commissioned in 1541 to commemorate the union of the two companies.*

FACING PAGE (below right): *Thomas Cromwell, the king's chief secretary from 1533, and vicar-general from 1535 until his fall and execution in 1540. He guided many reformatory statutes through parliament, and supervised the dissolution of the monasteries. He also helped Cranmer to obtain royal authorisation for the English translation of the bible.*

FACING PAGE (below left): *Thomas Howard, 3rd Duke of Norfolk. He served Henry capably as a soldier, but found his political ambitions repeatedly frustrated. The rashness of his son, the poet Surrey, almost brought him to the scaffold, but the king's death saved him.*

HENRICO OCTAVO OPT MAX REGI ANGLIÆ
FRANCIÆ ET HIBERNIÆ FIDEI DEFENSO
RI AC ANGLICANÆ HIBERNICÆQ
ECCLESIÆ PROXIME A CHRISTO SVPREMO
CAPITI SOCIETAS CHIRVRGORVM
COMMVNIBVS VOTIS HÆC CONSECRAT

TRISTIOR ANGLORVM PESTIS VIOLAVERAT ORBEM
INFESTANS ANIMOS CORPORIBVSQVE SEDENS
HANC DEVS INSIGNEM CLADEM MISERATVS AB ALTO
TE MEDICI MVNVS IVSSIT OBIRE BONI
LVMEN EVANGELII FVLVIS CIRCVMVOLAT ALIS
PHARMACON ADFECTIS MENTIBVS ILLVD ERIT
CONSILIOQ TVO CELEBRANT MONVMENTA GALENI
ET SELERI MORBVS PELLITVR OMNIS OPE
NOS IGITVR SVPPLEX MEDICORVM TVRBA TVORVM
HANC TIBI SACRAMVS RELIGIONE DOMVM
MVNERIS ET MEMORES QVO NOS HENRICE BEASTI
IMPERIO OPTAMVS MAXIMA QVLQVE TVO

BVTTS
I CHAMBER
T VICARY
I AYLEF
N SYMSON
E HARMAN
X SAMON
W TYLLY
I PEN
N ALCOKE

had monopolised in the previous decade, he eventually offered his hand to Anne, the sister of the young duke of Cleves. Though the duke was not himself a Lutheran, he was allied by marriage and by political interest with the house of Saxony, and through it with the wider league of German Lutheran princes. In 1539, since the emperor and the king of France had for the time being patched up their interminable quarrel, and the pope, Paul III, had seized the opportunity to declare his sentence of excommunication against Henry to be now in force, there was a real danger that the Catholic monarchs might combine forces in an attack on schismatic England. Against such a threat the German Lutherans offered virtually the only possible counter-alliance.

The negotiation of a marriage treaty was, however, always a lengthy business, and by the time the arrangements for the Cleves marriage were complete, and Anne had come to England to meet and marry Henry, the need for the alliance which she represented was already passing. We need not accept as gospel truth all the unflattering things which Henry was later reported to have said about Anne in order to establish that he had never been able to bring himself to consummate his marriage with her, but we must accept that she did not fire his blood, and that once the diplomatic situation shifted in England's favour he saw no reason why he should remain tied to her for life. Anne was very sensible about it all. She made no attempt to resist the king's will or to fight for her rights. By her wise complaisance she earned for herself the title of "King's sister" and a very comfortable endowment.

The story of Henry's fifth wife, Catherine Howard, is in many ways a repetition of that of Anne Boleyn. At the age of 49, and already talking of himself as an old man, Henry's passions were aroused and his spirits rejuvenated by the appearance of this girl of less than twenty. The king could not find words to express his admiration and joy when she consented to be his wife. She was his jewel of womanhood, his perfect partner, and much else besides. She was also, as Anne Boleyn before her, a niece of the duke of Norfolk and the repository of the hopes of a political faction. She had been very deliberately put in the king's way by her uncle and bishop Stephen Gardiner who were working to destroy the influence of Thomas Cromwell and to reassert their own. Anne Boleyn in her day had helped the promotion of many supporters of the Reformation, notably Thomas Cranmer. Catherine, they hoped, would in similar fashion be an asset to the conservative interest which they represented. Though Cromwell fell before the king divorced Anne of Cleves and married Catherine Howard, there is no doubt that the latter played an important part in bringing about this palace revolution.

Catherine thoroughly enjoyed her new position and the power and riches it put into her hands. She eagerly accepted the many lavish gifts bestowed upon her by the infatuated king, but she did not (how could she be expected to?) return his love and preferred, in a most dangerously indiscreet manner, to keep up contact with the men friends of her unmarried days. This was to be her undoing, more dramatically and more swiftly than in the case of her cousin Anne

Boleyn. In November 1541, less than sixteen months after her marriage, a dossier of her indiscretions, prepared by her enemies, was put in the hands of the king by Cranmer. At first Henry affected to take little notice, but for form's sake started some enquiries. Before long the whole truth came out and the king's wrath was terrible. The idol was shattered; the dream became a nightmare; he had been most cruelly deceived by this flighty and unprincipled slut. He who had defied both pope and emperor had been made to look a fool. The very worst aspect of Catherine's behaviour was her total failure to show a proper respect for her royal husband who now, in his own realm, stood "next only unto God" in authority over all his people. For this, as much as for her alleged infidelities, Catherine had to die.

Henry's last wife, the one who survived him, Catherine Parr, was altogether more circumspect and deferential in her behaviour. She was much older, and very much more experienced, than her unfortunate predecessor. When she married Henry on 12 June 1542 she was thirty-one and had already had two husbands, the second having been one of the leaders of the great rebellion of 1536 which is known as the Pilgrimage of Grace. She married the king with her eyes open. She knew well the dangers as well as the advantages of being Henry's queen, but she was wise

* * *

ABOVE RIGHT: *Catherine Howard, Henry's fifth queen. She was a young and vivacious bride for the ageing king and he felt quite rejuvenated by her. No fully authentic portrait of this queen survives.*

RIGHT: *A portrait of Catherine Parr, sixth wife of Henry VIII, attributed to William Scrots. Catherine married Henry, her third husband, in 1542, and after his death she obtained Edward VI's consent to her marriage to Sir Thomas Seymour.*

FACING PAGE: *The title page of the Great Bible, 1541 edition. The king hands copies of the Bible to Cranmer (left) and Cromwell (right) for distribution to the clergy and laity. As Cromwell had been executed in the previous year, it was necessary to erase his arms—hence the blank roundel at his feet.*

enough not to oppose his imperious will, and skilful enough to know how to ease his suffering and to turn aside his wrath. In the closing years of the reign, while the political vultures gathered round the diseased body of the ageing king, and jostled each other for position, only she, and to a lesser degree Cranmer, brought any touch of humanity and charity to the faction-ridden court. She was a cultured woman, and was very much in sympathy with the Protestant reformers, but was wise enough not to appear too openly to be their partisan. Her influence was probably crucial in securing as tutors for prince Edward men who were not only the foremost English scholars of the day, but were also to reveal their Protestant sympathies just as soon as it was safe for them to do so, that is immediately after Henry's death.

On 28 January 1547 death came at last to Henry VIII who, during the course of his long reign, had sent so many others to the scaffold. Long after his doctors had despaired of his recovery his courtiers were unable to bring themselves to tell him to prepare for death, so mortally afraid of his anger were they to the very end. Consequently Cranmer, whom alone of all men the king really trusted because of his patent lack of ambition and all-embracing charity, was almost too late to administer comfort to his dying sovereign. Henry was past speech when the archbishop came to him, and could only press his hand in token of his faith. He left his kingdom, the kingdom for whose external security and internal peace he believed he had exerted himself to the utmost of his ability all of his days, to a boy of nine.

The great achievement of Henry's reign, view it how you will, was the cementing together of his kingdom under the unchallenged and all-embracing power of the crown. All else had been ancillary to this. The rejection of the papal supremacy had followed on, as we have seen, from the king's concern with his marriage and the succession, but a showdown between the king and the pope was probably inevitable in any case, and might well have arisen out of some other matter. Henry could not abide any rival in his realm. The Church in England would have to acknowledge his authority as effectively as did the parliament and other institutions of the state. Those who presumed to set themselves up as rivals to the king, be they native peers or alien bishops, were all struck down with equal vigour. The crown alone emerged triumphant, but by the time the process was at an end it was often impossible to distinguish the interest of the crown from the selfish will of a bloated tyrant.

* * *

ABOVE: *Portrait of Henry VIII by Hans Holbein the Younger (1494–1543). This picture painted on a wooden panel shows the king in the last years of his life. It now hangs in the Blue Boudoir at Warwick Castle.*

★

ACKNOWLEDGMENTS

With the exception of the following, all the illustrations in this book are from the Royal Collection and are reproduced by gracious permission of H.M. The Queen: pp. ii cover, 4 top right and bottom, 5, 7, 11, 12, 14 top left, 15, 16 bottom left, 21 bottom right, 23 bottom, by courtesy of the National Portrait Gallery, London; p. i cover, Walker Art Gallery, Liverpool; p. 1, Sudeley Castle, Gloucestershire; p. 2, Ashmolean Museum, Oxford; pp. 6 top, 22, British Library; p.6 bottom, University College, London; p. 14 top right, by kind permission of the Master and Fellows of Trinity Hall, Cambridge; p. 14 bottom, Vatican Library; p. 18, The Louvre, Paris; p. 19, Galleria Nazionale dell'arte antica, Rome; p. 21 top, The Barber-Surgeons Company; p. 24, by permission of the Earl of Warwick.

ISBN 0 85372 073 8